LIN TERNET

ESSENTIAL TIPS

Using the

INTERNET

TECHNICAL CONSULTANTS
Peter Jackson and Chris Lewis

DK

DORLING KINDERSLEY
London • New York • Sydney
www.dk.com

A DORLING KINDERSLEY BOOK
www.dk.com

Editor May Corfield
Art Editor Bill Mason
Senior Editor Gillian Roberts
Series Art Editor Alison Donovan
Production Controller Wendy Penn

The full names of certain products referred to in this book are: Microsoft® MS-DOS®, Microsoft® Windows® 98, MSN™, The Microsoft® Network, Microsoft® Internet Gaming Zone, Microsoft® Internet Explorer, Netscape Communications, the Netscape Communications logo, Netscape & Netscape Navigator are trademarks of Netscape Communications Corporation. RealNetworks, RealAudio, RealPlayer, WebActive and the RN logo are registered trademarks of RealNetworks, Inc.
Every effort has been made to trace the copyright holders. The publisher apologizes for any unintentional omissions and would be pleased, in such cases, to place an acknowledgment in future editions of this book.

Second edition first published in Great Britain in 1999 by
Dorling Kindersley Limited,
9 Henrietta Street, London WC2E 8PS

A CIP catalogue record for this book is available from the British Library

ISBN 0-7513-2690-9

Reproduced by Colourscan, Singapore
Printed and bound by Graphicom, Italy

ESSENTIAL TIPS
101

UNDERSTANDING THE INTERNET

1 WHAT IS THE INTERNET?

The Internet is a worldwide network of computers, holding vast quantities of data that you can access directly from a PC. Access to the Internet is channelled through the high-speed links provided by commercial organizations known as service providers. Although the volume and variety of information may seem overwhelming, the basic processes are quite straightforward: you do not need to be a computer expert to enjoy the Internet.

Files & software that are publicly available on the Internet can be accessed and downloaded using FTP (File Transfer Protocol).

Electronic Mail (e-mail) is a fast and economical way to send messages to anyone with an Internet account. Messages can include text, pictures, and even audio or animation.

YOUR PLACE IN THE NET
Once you have connected your PC to a modem and signed up with a service provider, you can select which software to use and start exploring the Net. As you become more experienced, you will discover which areas appeal to you most.

An individual can access data and communicate with others worldwide from their PC.

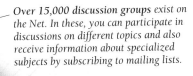

Over 15,000 discussion groups exist on the Net. In these, you can participate in discussions on different topics and also receive information about specialized subjects by subscribing to mailing lists.

Numerous colourful sites make up the World Wide Web: Web browser software lets you navigate around them. Many Web pages are interactive, allowing you to move from one site to another by clicking on a "hot" word or icon.

On-line chatting, where individuals are able to to communicate "live" with each other via their computer keyboards, is a hugely popular activity on the Internet.

Users receive their link to the Internet, e-mail addresses, and telephone access numbers from one or more of the thousands of commercial service providers.

② IS IT WORLDWIDE?

Although, technically, anyone with a PC and modem can telephone a service provider and access the Net, some countries have few service providers and limited local coverage. Access also depends, to some extent, on the sophistication of a country's telephone system.

3 WHAT CAN YOU DO ON THE INTERNET?

Once you are connected to the Internet, you join a global community of over 50 million users with whom you can communicate "live" or by sending e-mail messages; you can subscribe to newsgroups or mailing lists, and engage in on-line shopping; and you can access any of the huge amount of electronic data that is stored on the computers that make up the Internet.

△ VISITING INTERNET SITES
Using a Web browser such as Netscape Navigator, *it is easy to visit Internet sites: just type the address and press the Return key.*

△ WEB BROWSERS
Although Web browsers were originally designed for accessing Web pages, today's powerful versions are more versatile and provide newcomers with an excellent method of exploring the Internet.

△ SURFING BETWEEN SITES
On any Web page, click an underlined link to move to another page on the same site, or to switch to a different site.

4 UNDERSTANDING NETWORKS

At the Internet's core is a network of supercomputers (represented on the illustration by red dots), which are connected to each other by high-speed links (the white lines) known as "backbones". Each node is linked to a number of smaller networks, which are linked, in turn, to even smaller networks, and so, ultimately, to your PC.

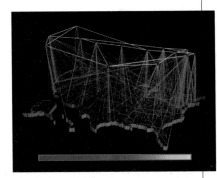

THE MAIN US NETWORK — NSFNET

5 ESSENTIAL JARGON

Newcomers to the Internet are often bewildered by the acronyms, abbreviations, and the seemingly incomprehensible terminology that abounds. Below is a glossary of some of the most common terms.

- **Anonymous FTP**
A way of logging on to a remote computer using an FTP program.

- **Archie**
A database of files stored on FTP sites.

- **BBS**
A single computer or network that you dial direct to access services (*Tip 18*).

- **Client/Server**
Computers within a network are either clients, which request information, or servers, which store and deliver information.

- **FTP**
A protocol for transferring files on the Internet (*Tip 37*).

- **IRC**
Networks on the Net where you hold "live" conversations with other users.

- **ISDN**
A communication standard allowing a telephone line to carry digital data at speeds higher than is possible with a modem (*Tip 6*).

- **Newbie**
A user who is new to the Internet.

- **PoP**
The telephone number that customers use to dial in to their service provider.

- **URL (Uniform Resource Locator)**
An Internet address, providing a standard way of referring to Internet resources.

- **Usenet**
The main network of newsgroups available on the Internet.

- **Web browser**
A program for viewing and accessing data on the World Wide Web.

GETTING CONNECTED

6 WHAT IS NEEDED TO GET CONNECTED?

To connect to the Internet you need a computer (any fairly new computer should be suitable, as long as it has enough power and memory); a modem to convert data so it can be transmitted over the telephone network; and an account with a service provider to provide the link between your computer and the Internet. The software will come either with the computer or from the service provider.

WHAT IS ISDN?
The Integrated Services Digital Network lets you send digital information at very high speeds over existing telephone lines, providing the fastest link to the Internet. However, you need a special telephone connection and can use it only if your service provider also has an ISDN link.

EXTERNAL MODEM

▽ ALL-IN-ONE INTERNET KITS
Starter kits are popular with beginners and usually contain a modem, cable and adapter, software, and a manual. Some kits also include a free trial account with a reputable service provider.

Cable

Fax modem

Modem software

7 MINIMUM PC REQUIREMENTS

Although many people access the Internet with relatively slow computers, you will need a faster model to explore effectively the features described in this book – an IBM-compatible PC with at least a Pentium processor and 32 (but preferably 64) MB RAM.

8 CHECK THE SPEED OF YOUR SERIAL PORT

To use a fast external modem effectively, you need a buffered transceiver chip such as a 16550 in your PC's serial port. With a slower unbuffered chip, the maximum speed of the modem-to-computer connection is reduced. Most modern PCs will have a 16550 or equivalent in each serial port, but it is worth checking that the chip is working.

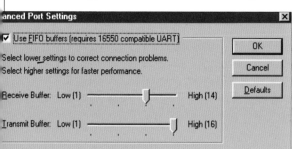

◁ **CHECK SERIAL PORT HARDWARE**
- *Use PC's Setup software to check that the serial ports have 16550 chips.*
- *Double-click on Modems in Windows 98 Control Panel.*
- *Check that the Use FIFO buffers option is ticked.*

9 HOW A MODEM WORKS

A modem (the term is simply a contraction of Modulator-Demodulator) is a device that converts data from the binary code used by your computer to an analogue signal that can be transmitted over the telephone network, and vice versa.

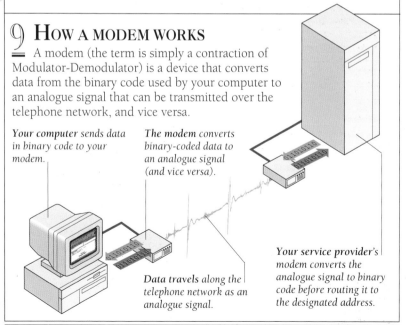

Your computer sends data in binary code to your modem.

The modem converts binary-coded data to an analogue signal (and vice versa).

Data travels along the telephone network as an analogue signal.

Your service provider's modem converts the analogue signal to binary code before routing it to the designated address.

10 CHOOSING A MODEM

Modems exist in a variety of shapes and sizes, but the basic choice is between external, internal, and card versions. After deciding which of those is most suited to your needs, consider price, speed, and compatibility. PC and Internet magazines are a good source of reviews and information about what is currently available.

FAX MODEMS
Most modems come with software to send and receive faxes, and fax facilities are also built into program suites like Microsoft Office as well as electronic mail.

△ EXTERNAL MODEM
Simple to connect, external modems are available in many different designs.

△ CARD MODEM
Ideal for installation in a notebook PC, this modem is the size of a credit card.

△ INTERNAL MODEM
An internal modem fits into an expansion slot inside your computer.

11 WHEN IS MODEM SPEED IMPORTANT?

Although the importance of speed depends on how you plan to use your modem, it is generally advisable to buy the fastest model you can afford. This is especially true if you intend to explore the World Wide Web and to download a lot of files. Modem speed is also an important factor in reducing your on-line telephone charges.

12 INTERNAL OR EXTERNAL MODEM?

There are several factors you need to consider when choosing a modem. Bear in mind that it can be a complicated business to install an internal modem, so if you are new to PCs or an inexperienced user, an external modem (which is simple to connect) may be the best choice.
▪ An internal modem takes up no desk space, and needs no cable or electrical socket.

▪ An external modem needs cable and electrical socket, but is easy to move to another PC. The indicator lights let you see the status of your Internet session, and a speaker lets you hear a connection being made.

EXTERNAL MODEM

13 CONNECTING AN INTERNAL MODEM

If you are a beginner, do not try to install an internal modem yourself; ask your dealer to do it. An internal modem is a card that is fitted into a vacant expansion slot on your computer's motherboard. After installation of an internal modem card, it may be necessary to adjust the *Windows 98* settings if 'plug and play' installation fails.

14 CONNECTING AN EXTERNAL MODEM

Connecting an external modem is usually a straightforward task. First, connect your modem to the power supply, using the cable provided; this may include a power adapter. Now attach one end of the serial cable to the modem, and the other end to a vacant serial port on your PC; this will usually be the COM 1 port, but if a mouse is already connected there, use COM 2. Finally, plug the telephone cable into a telephone socket and switch on the modem. Some of the indicator lights should light up.

SERIAL
CABLE

△ SERIAL CABLE ADAPTER
An adapter cable or plug converts a 25-pin plug to fit a 9-pin socket.

AVOID SCREECHING
External modems can emit an unpleasant screeching sound when establishing connections. Avoid this by choosing a modem with a built-in volume control.

◁ AC POWER ADAPTER
Your modem may have a built-in power cable, with adapter; otherwise, plug the cable in with a jack.

15 How to Configure a Modem in Windows® 98

Having connected an external modem to your PC, you can now configure it in *Windows 98*. First, make sure that the modem is connected to a power supply and switched on (at least one of the display lights should be lit), then follow the steps below. Although it is possible for *Windows 98* to detect automatically the make and model of your modem, it is simple to do it manually.

1 △ From *Start* button, go to *Settings* and then to *Control Panel*.

2 △ Double-click on *Modems* icon; *Install New Modem* window will now appear.

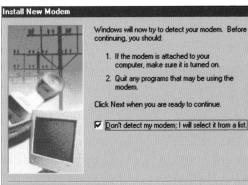

Install New Modem

Windows will now try to detect your modem. Before continuing, you should:

1. If the modem is attached to your computer, make sure it is turned on.

2. Quit any programs that may be using the modem.

Click Next when you are ready to continue.

☑ Don't detect my modem; I will select it from a list.

< Back   Next >   Cancel

3 △ Read and follow instructions in box, then check box next to *Don't detect my modem; I will select it from a list*. Now click *Next*.

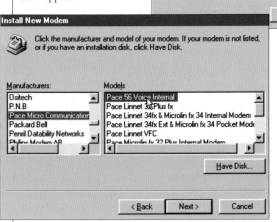

Install New Modem

Click the manufacturer and model of your modem. If your modem is not listed, or if you have an installation disk, click Have Disk.

Manufacturers:
- Ositech
- P.N.B
- Pace Micro Communication
- Packard Bell
- Penril Datability Networks
- Phyline Modem AB

Models:
- Pace 56 Voice Internal
- Pace Linnet 3x Plus fx
- Pace Linnet 34fx & Microlin fx 34 Internal Modem
- Pace Linnet 34fx Ext & Microlin fx 34 Pocket Mode
- Pace Linnet VFC
- Pace Microlin fx 32 Plus Internal Modem

Have Disk...

< Back   Next >   Cancel

4 ◁ Using vertical scroll bars, select appropriate make and model of your modem in *Manufacturers* box and then in *Models* box. Click *Next*.

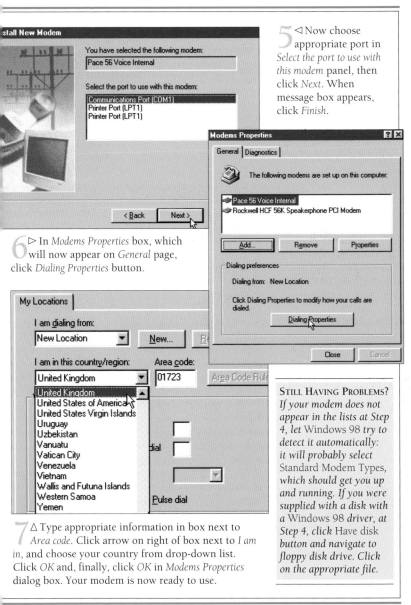

stall New Modem

You have selected the following modem:

Pace 56 Voice Internal

Select the port to use with this modem:

Communications Port (COM1)
Printer Port (LPT1)
Printer Port (LPT1)

< Back   Next >

5 ◁ Now choose appropriate port in *Select the port to use with this modem* panel, then click *Next*. When message box appears, click *Finish*.

Modems Properties ? X

General | Diagnostics |

The following modems are set up on this computer:

Pace 56 Voice Internal
Rockwell HCF 56K Speakerphone PCI Modem

Add...   Remove   Properties

Dialing preferences

Dialing from: New Location

Click Dialing Properties to modify how your calls are dialed.

Dialing Properties

Close   Cancel

6 ▷ In *Modems Properties* box, which will now appear on *General* page, click *Dialing Properties* button.

My Locations |

I am dialing from:

New Location ▼   New...   R

I am in this country/region: Area code:

United Kingdom ▼   01723   Area Code Rule

United Kingdom
United States of America
United States Virgin Islands
Uruguay
Uzbekistan
Vanuatu
Vatican City
Venezuela
Vietnam
Wallis and Futuna Islands
Western Samoa
Yemen

dial

Pulse dial

7 △ Type appropriate information in box next to *Area code*. Click arrow on right of box next to *I am in*, and choose your country from drop-down list. Click *OK* and, finally, click *OK* in *Modems Properties* dialog box. Your modem is now ready to use.

STILL HAVING PROBLEMS?
If your modem does not appear in the lists at Step 4, let Windows 98 *try to detect it automatically: it will probably select* Standard Modem Types, *which should get you up and running. If you were supplied with a disk with a* Windows 98 *driver, at Step 4, click* Have disk *button and navigate to floppy disk drive. Click on the appropriate file.*

16 TELEPHONE TIPS

If you use the "call waiting" facility with your telephone, you must disable it before commencing a modem session, as the beep that announces an incoming call could disrupt data transfer. To do this, check the box next to *To disable call waiting, dial* in the *Dialing Properties* dialog box (Steps 6 & 7, Tip 15). You'll have to contact your telephone company to find out what to put in the box, or choose from the drop-down menu.

DISABLE CALL WAITING

Contents | Index | Search

- ? Welcome to Help
- Introducing Windows 98
- Exploring Your Computer
- Exploring the Internet
- Using Windows Accessories
- Printing
- Managing Hardware and Software
- Connecting to Networks
- Using Accessibility Features
- Getting Started Book: Online Version
- Troubleshooting
  - ? Using Windows 98 troubleshoot
  - Contact Microsoft Technical Sup
  - Windows 98 Troubleshooters

MODEM TROUBLESHOOTING

17 MODEM HELP & ADVICE

The *Windows 98* help system provides some useful on-line advice on modem problems. If you have difficulties with installation, access *Windows Help* and look for *modems* in the Index.

■ To deal with other problems, first choose *Help* from the *Start* menu, click *Troubleshooting* in the *Contents* page, and then click on *Modem* in the *Windows 98 Troubleshooters* section.

■ Your modem supplier should be able to advise you about *Windows 98*-compatible modem drivers.

---

18 DIAL A BBS TO TEST YOUR MODEM

Once you have installed and configured your modem, you can test it by dialling a Bulletin Board Service. All you need is a telephone number for a BBS (these are often advertised in PC magazines) and the *Windows 98* accessory called *HyperTerminal*. Many BBSs are commercial concerns, but others are free services run by enthusiasts.

19 CONNECT TO A BBS WITH HYPERTERMINAL

The first time you make a BBS connection, *HyperTerminal* will prompt you for information about dialling properties and modem settings, enabling you to assign an icon and a name to each connection. Future connections can then be made by double-clicking the relevant icon in the

1 ◁ From *Start* menu choose *Programs* then select *Accessories*. Double-click *Hypertrm* icon in *HyperTerminal* window.

Hypertrm

HyperTerminal window. Install *HyperTerminal* from your *Windows 98* installation CD or disks, using the *Add/Remove Programs* utility.

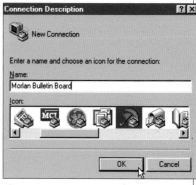

2 △ In *Connection Description* dialog box, type name of BBS you wish to call in *Name* box. Click an icon in *Icon* box. Click *OK*. Icon and name will now appear in *HyperTerminal* window.

3 ◁ In *Phone Number* dialog box, choose relevant country code, then type area code and telephone number for Bulletin Board Service you wish to call. Click *OK*. A *Connect* box will appear. Click *Dial* to connect to BBS.

20 ACCESSING THE INTERNET

To gain access to the Internet, you must first open an account with a service (or access) provider. There are many such companies, each offering slightly different services, and some are free.

There are two main categories: Internet Service Providers and On-line Service Providers (*Tips 21 & 22*). Both offer Internet access, but the latter also provides exclusive information and services.

21 INTERNET SERVICE PROVIDERS

There are dozens of Internet Service Providers, offering a range of services. The most recent trend is for ISPs to offer free unlimited Internet access using free software on CD-ROM, with users paying only the cost of local-rate telephone calls. Using this model, *Dixon's Freeserve* already has more than a million users. However, other ISPs charging a monthly fee can still compete by providing premium extra services like Web site hosting and domain name registration.

WHAT IS A PoP?
PoPs are local telephone access numbers offered by service providers. The extent of PoP coverage offered varies greatly, and this is a factor to consider when deciding which provider to sign up with. If you can dial a PoP at local call rates, you will be able to use the Internet at that rate.

INTERNET ACCESS
If your ISP offers direct Internet connection, you can run any Internet software, such as the latest Web browsers.

ON-LINE CHARGES
Some Internet Service Providers charge a flat monthly or annual fee that gives you unlimited access to the Internet, with no extra charges.

PoP COVERAGE
The major ISPs usually provide excellent PoP coverage in their own countries, but access from abroad may be difficult.

NO EXTRA CONTENT
Internet Service Providers offer no extra content: they simply provide access to the Internet as a whole, which you then use as you wish.

22 ON-LINE SERVICE PROVIDERS

The main commercial On-line Service Providers, such as *MSN* and *America Online (AOL)*, offer vast databases of information. Services include news, weather, and software support, as well as simple access to the Internet via a number of easy-to-follow screens. The trend among On-line Service Providers such as *AOL*, which has the greatest number of subscribers, is to adopt a flat-rate pricing model, charging a fixed monthly rate for unlimited hours on-line.

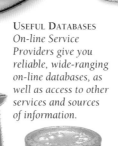

INTERNET ACCESS
Easy access to the Internet is built in to the software provided, so you can, for example, launch a Web browser or access an FTP site simply by clicking a button.

USEFUL DATABASES
On-line Service Providers give you reliable, wide-ranging on-line databases, as well as access to other services and sources of information.

ON-LINE CHARGES
Although precise charges and billing procedures vary, the trend is for On-line Service Providers to charge a fixed monthly rate for unlimited usage.

POP COVERAGE
The major On-line Service Providers are US-based and offer worldwide PoP coverage, so it is simple to access your account when not at home.

23 TRY BEFORE YOU BUY

Free trial accounts are frequently offered – as part of a modem package, for example, or on CD-ROMs given away by computer magazines. These offer a way of trying out different service providers before signing up. Be sure to check the small print carefully, however, to avoid being billed for use after the trial period.

△ FREE TRIAL ACCOUNT OFFERS

◁ INTERNET CAFÉS
Sometimes known as cybercafés, these provide an excellent opportunity to find out what the Internet has to offer and to experiment with the services available. Experts are on hand to assist you, and training courses are usually available.

CYBERIA CAFÉ, PARIS

24 ASK BEFORE SIGNING UP

Get as much information as possible before signing up with a service provider. Below are some of the important questions to ask.

How much will it cost?
- What is the registration fee, if any?
- Does the monthly fee give unlimited Internet access?

What software is provided?
- Web browser, FTP program, e-mail program, newsreader?
- Will the software be registered to me?
- Will the software install itself automatically?

Do you offer PPP (Point to Point Protocol) for Internet connection?

What is the extent of PoP coverage?
- Is there a local PoP?
- Is national PoP coverage extensive?

What support do you offer?
- When are your telephone support lines open?

What sort of e-mail account will I have?
- Do you offer POP3 (allows access from any computer) or SMTP (Simple Mail Transfer Protocol) facilities? What would my e-mail address be?

CHECK COSTS

SENDING & RECEIVING E-MAIL

25 WHAT IS ELECTRONIC MAIL?

Using electronic mail (e-mail), you can send messages to anyone with an Internet account, and most businesses today have an electronic mailing address. Your e-mail message can include not just text but other files, such as images and spreadsheets. An even greater advantage is that your message can reach the recipient within minutes of being sent. Incoming messages are stored in your mailbox on your service provider's mail server until you next connect to the Internet.

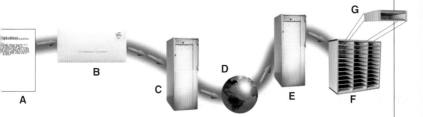

There are many ways of sending and receiving electronic mail, but the basic process is the same. **A** Using a suitable e-mail program, you type your message. **B** Once you have addressed and sent your e-mail, it is encoded by a modem and sent down the telephone line as an analogue signal. **C** The e-mail message arrives at your provider's server; if it recognizes the e-mail address as valid, the e-mail is sent. **D** The data is sent via the Internet. **E** The data is received by the recipient's provider and sent to his or her unique "pigeon hole". **F** Once your message reaches the host, it will remain there until the recipient next connects to the Internet. **G** Finally, the recipient's modem and computer decode the data and your e-mail message can be read as a text file.

E-MAIL ADDRESSES
The following Web sites list many addresses:
http://www.bigfoot.com
http://people.yahoo.com
http://www.infospace.
co.uk

26 HOW TO DECIPHER AN E-MAIL ADDRESS

An e-mail address has two parts: the user name and a domain name, separated by an @ symbol. The number of domains in a name depends on how many branches are needed to sort it logically. Each address is unique, and must be used exactly as given; adding spaces or changing from lower to upper case, or vice versa, may render it useless.

Your user name can be any name you choose, as long as it has not already been registered by another subscriber. You could use your full name, your first name, or an alias. Some service providers allocate numbers instead of names.

Your host name is the name of your Internet Service Provider, the organization that provides you with Internet access and is responsible for sending and receiving messages to and from individual users.

The last section of the domain name identifies your service provider's type of organization, and this may vary from one country to another. For example, in the US, .com indicates a commercial company, whereas the UK equivalent is .co.

USER **DOMAINS**

bsimpson @ provider . com .co.uk

The @ symbol separates your user name from the domain name part of the address, which relates to your service provider.

The • symbol separates the various domains of your address. Note that there is no space between the dot and adjacent letters.

A two-letter country code forms the last part of the domain name of service providers based outside the US. For example, jp for Japan and fr for France.

27 PROTECTING CONFIDENTIALITY

Be cautious about sending sensitive or confidential information via e-mail, since the contents could be read by anyone with access to the recipient's computer. If this is of concern, seek professional advice about the possibility of protecting your mail with special software.

28 DEDICATED E-MAIL PROGRAMS

There are many different ways of sending and receiving e-mail, including several dedicated e-mail programs. Qualcomm's *Eudora*, one of the most widely used programs, is available in a freeware version (*Eudora Light*) from Qualcomm's site at **www.eudora.com**.

29 SETTING UP E-MAIL

To set up e-mail using *Outlook Express,*
you need a POP3 account – a specific type of
e-mail transfer protocol used by most service
providers. If you are unsure about the type of
e-mail account you have, check with your
provider. When you first run *Outlook Express,*
you will be asked to provide some configuration
details, including your e-mail address and the
name of your service provider's mail server. Find
Outlook Express from the programs section of the
Start menu and follow these steps.

1 △ Select *Outlook Express* and the *Internet Connection Wizard* will appear ready for your mail details.

2 ◁ If you already have an e-mail address, type it in the appropriate box.

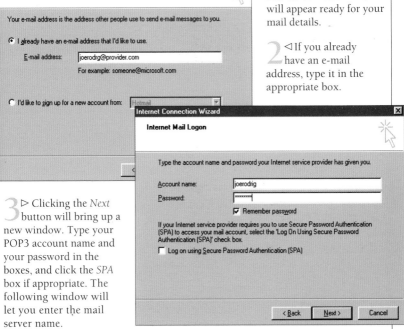

3 ▷ Clicking the *Next* button will bring up a new window. Type your POP3 account name and your password in the boxes, and click the *SPA* box if appropriate. The following window will let you enter the mail server name.

30 SEND AN E-MAIL WITH OUTLOOK EXPRESS

Once you have configured the basic program settings, all you need to know is the e-mail address of the person to whom you wish to send a message. After making your Internet connection, launch *Outlook Express*, then follow the steps below, which explain how to write and send a message while on-line. (You can also write an e-mail off-line and send it later.)

1 △ Click *New Mail* button. A blank *New Message* will appear for you to compose and address your mail.

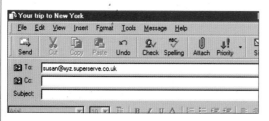

2 ◁ In *New Message* window, place cursor alongside "To". Type e-mail address of recipient (normally in lower case letters). Press Tab key twice to put cursor next to "Subject".

3 ▷ In Subject line, type brief description of subject; this becomes the new window title. Press Tab and type message.

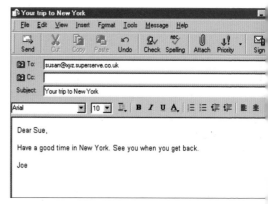

Dear Sue,

Have a good time in New York. See you when you get back.

Joe

4 △ When ready to send your message, click *Send* button.

WRITING MAIL OFF-LINE
If you process a lot of mail, write your messages off-line and place them in a queue (by pressing Send *while off-line). When you are next on-line, send all messages by clicking the* Send/Recv *button in main* Outlook *window.*

31 ATTACHING A DOCUMENT

Many e-mail programs allow you to send files from your hard disk by "attaching" them to your message. If you wish to use this facility to attach a document to your message when you are using *Outlook Express*, click the *Attach* button or choose *File Attachment* from the *Insert* menu before you click on *Send*. This opens a dialog box and lets you locate, on your hard disk, the document you wish to attach to your message.

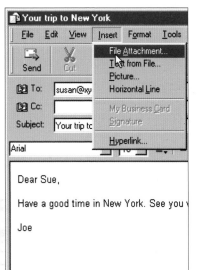

ATTACH A FILE

If a recipient is unable to view an attachment you have sent, ask which encoding method his or her e-mail program supports, because incompatibilities can occur. Three of the most common methods are MIME, UUEncode, and BINHEX.

SENDING FILES BY E-MAIL
If you send a lot of large files, save time by using a compression program.

32 CAN E-MAIL MESSAGES BE DELIVERED IF THE ADDRESS IS WRONG?

E-mail messages, like conventional mail, must be correctly addressed. If the computer trying to deliver your message does not recognize the mailing address, it will automatically send you a warning e-mail. You may see this message the next time you look in your mailbox, or perhaps several days later. In some systems, especially the on-line services, you can generate a receipt when your e-mail has been correctly delivered and read by the recipient.

HELPFUL DESCRIPTIONS
Try to get into the habit of supplying a helpful subject description each time you send an e-mail message, particularly if you are posting to a mailing list. This will help recipients to decide whether a message needs their urgent attention.

33 RECEIVING E-MAIL WITH OUTLOOK EXPRESS

Outlook Express can be configured to alert you each time new mail arrives (as long as you are on-line). Choose *Options* from the *Tools* menu, then check that the box labelled *Play Sound When New Messages Arrive* is selected. You can also opt to send and receive messages automatically when the program is started, and change the frequency with which *Outlook Express* checks for new messages. To read messages, follow the steps below.

!	0	♈	From	Subject
			fred @client.co.uk	Our meeting next week
			sue @abc.superserve.co.uk	I'm back

1 △ Click on the *Inbox* button to display all messages received, both read and unread.

2 △ The *Inbox* display shows each message on a separate line, with the sender's e-mail address, the Subject line, and the date and time received.

3 ▷ Double-clicking on a message opens a new window displaying it, with the Subject as window title. The message can also contain graphics.

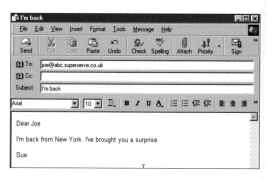

34 HOW TO REPLY TO AN E-MAIL MESSAGE

To answer an e-mail message, click on the *Reply* button in the message window. This will produce a new message window with the original text highlighted and indented. You can include the original text in your reply to remind the recipient of what they had originally sent.

E-MAIL MESSAGE & REPLY

35 STORING E-MAIL ADDRESSES

Most e-mail programs have an address-book facility for storing and managing your list of e-mail addresses. The address book in *Outlook Express* allows you to select addresses from an alphabetical list.

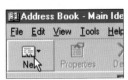

Address Book - Main Ide
File Edit View Tools Help
New Properties De

1 △ To add a new entry, click on the *New* button in the Address Book window and choose the *New Contact* option.

2 ◁ In the *Properties* window, enter the name, e-mail address, nickname, title, and any extra notes.

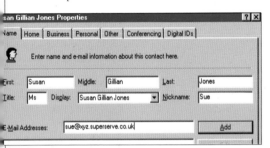

san Gillian Jones Properties ? ✕
Name | Home | Business | Personal | Other | Conferencing | Digital IDs |

Enter name and e-mail information about this contact here.

First: Susan   Middle: Gillian   Last: Jones
Title: Ms   Display: Susan Gillian Jones ▼   Nickname: Sue

E-Mail Addresses: sue@xyz.superserve.co.uk   Add

SETTING THROUGH OPTIONS
Choosing Options *in the* Tools *menu lets you configure every aspect of the program. In the* Send *section you can add to the* Address Book *the e-mail address of anybody to whom you reply.*

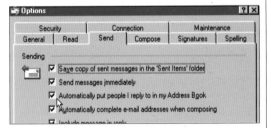

Options ? ✕
Security | Connection | Maintenance
General | Read | Send | Compose | Signatures | Spelling

Sending
☑ Save copy of sent messages in the 'Sent Items' folder
☑ Send messages immediately
☑ Automatically put people I reply to in my Address Book
☑ Automatically complete e-mail addresses when composing
☑ Include message in reply

36 USING ELECTRONIC MAILING LISTS

An electronic mailing list is a database of people who share an interest in a particular subject. Subscribers have thousands of different lists to choose from, and are automatically sent regular information by e-mail about their chosen subject. Each mailing list is managed by a remote computer, known as a listserver, which maintains a list of all users and their addresses, as well as receiving and passing on all e-mail messages contributed to the group.

DATABASE

DOWNLOADING
FILES

37 RETRIEVING FILES FROM THE INTERNET

To download any of the millions of files and programs available on the Internet, you can use either your Web browser or a process called File Transfer Protocol (FTP) to transfer them to your hard disk. ("Protocol" refers to a series of standard, predefined messages that allow a file to be retrieved, regardless of the type of computer you use.) Most users now use Web browsers for downloading, but an FTP utility should also have been supplied by your service provider.

△ CNET

NETSCAPE'S NETCENTER ▽

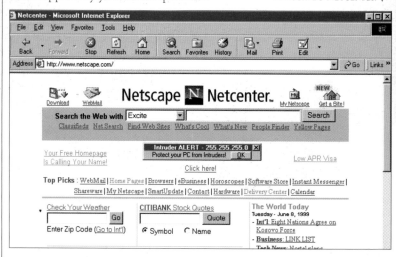

38 WHAT IS STORED IN FILES?

The Internet is a huge source of information that is accessible to individual subscribers across the globe. Any kind of information that can be stored on a computer – by individuals, educational or research establishments, governments, or by commercial organizations – is available: the quantity and range are almost beyond comprehension.

Documents abound in enormous quantities. The Gutenberg Project archive (at http://www.gutenberg.org), for example, holds thousands of complete electronic texts from Aesop's Fables *to* Zen and the Art of the Internet.

Software of almost any type is freely available for you to use indefinitely. For example, you can download many Windows 98 *drivers and updates from* http://support.microsoft.com.

Music, sounds, and speech of all descriptions are available from Web sites. For a collection of sound clips from the Star Trek *TV series, for example, visit* http://www.soundamerica.com.

Many images are available on Web sites, including photographs and video. There is a wonderful collection of NASA space photographs, for example, at http://www. nasa.gov/gallery/photo/index.html.

39 HOW DO YOU KNOW WHERE TO LOOK?

One of the biggest problems is that of finding out which files are actually available, and where to access them. One solution is to use specialized download sites like **http://www.winfiles.com** or **http://www.download.com**.

These provide simple access to as many files as they can, grouped by type. If you want to obtain software related to specific products, the manufacturer's Web site will usually have a download section for drivers and also some other utilities.

◁ WINFILES.COM
Winfiles.com stores a vast range of files of various types, covering everything for the Windows user.

DRIVERS ▷
A manufacturer's site can give quick access to the latest product drivers.

READ THE INSTRUCTIONS
When you log on to an FTP site, be sure to read the opening screens. Some FTP programs open "readme" screens automatically when you log on; others require you to choose to view them.

40 DOWNLOADING FILES USING FTP

For download sites without browser access, it is necessary to have an FTP program to transfer files from the host machine to your hard disk. Your service provider will probably have supplied an FTP program, but there are many alternatives available on the Internet if you would like to experiment.

41 CHOOSE AN FTP PROGRAM

Below are listed three of the most popular FTP programs.

- *CuteFTP*: A shareware program providing several sites that can be accessed from its FTP *Site Manager* window at **http://www.cuteftp.com**.
- *FTP Works*: A freeware program that is easy to use. More information is available on the Web at **http://www.corbanware.com**.
- *FTP Explorer*: With a similar interface to that of *Windows Explorer*, this program is currently free for noncommercial use and can be found at **http://www.ftpx.com**.

> **WINDOWS® 98 FTP PROGRAM**
> *Although more suited to advanced Internet users, the FTP program that is supplied with* Windows 98 *provides a simple command-line interface, where you type UNIX-style commands (similar to those used in Telnet). To run the program, choose* Run *from the* Start *menu and type* **ftp**.

42 WHAT IS "FREE" SOFTWARE?

The software that you can access and download from the Internet, although freely available, is not necessarily free. Be sure to check the conditions that apply to any file you download, as some software carries conditions that must be complied with legally. Most software includes a text file providing you with information about the author, the licence, and any action that you are required to take.

FREE SOFTWARE

Shareware
- Free to download.
- Free to try for a limited period.
- Protected by copyright.
- After trial period, you must stop using it, or register and pay a fee.

> **WHY REGISTER SHAREWARE?**
> *Registered versions usually include extra features, such as technical support and free upgrades. Your registration fee also helps fund further product development.*

Public Domain
- Free to download and use.
- Free from copyright protection.
- May be altered and used for profit.
- Must be explicitly declared as public domain by author; if not, assume that copyright applies.

Freeware
- Free to download and use.
- You do not need to register it.
- Protected by copyright.

43 DOWNLOADING FROM A BROWSER

You can download most files from Web sites through a browser program, by clicking on a button or a text link. The browser handles all the background protocols required, and can be set up to automatically decompress and install downloaded files. There is a wide variety of download sites on the Internet, from video clips to hardware drivers.

1 ▷ When you find a download site you like, it's a good idea to store its URL in *Internet Explorer's* list of Favorites, or as a *Netscape* bookmark. Keeping a list in a folder helps you find them easily.

2 ◁ This site at *http://www. winfiles.com* collects every kind of file to do with every variety of *Microsoft Windows*. The opening screen lets you pick the particular area in which you are interested.

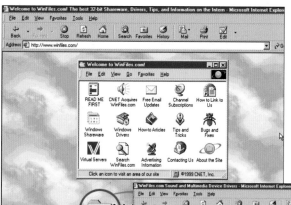

3 ▷ Clicking on *Windows Drivers*, and choosing the *Sound and Multimedia* section, brings up an alphabetical list of suppliers with links to driver download sources. Find your hardware here.

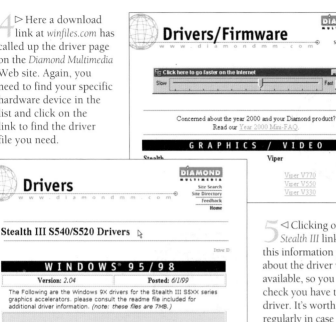

4 ▷ Here a download link at *winfiles.com* has called up the driver page on the *Diamond Multimedia* Web site. Again, you need to find your specific hardware device in the list and click on the link to find the driver file you need.

5 ◁ Clicking on the *Stealth III* link calls up this information page about the driver versions available, so you can check you have the right driver. It's worth checking regularly in case the driver has been upgraded.

6 ◁ Clicking on the download link starts to download the file. A warning box lets you choose to save the file or run it from the Web server; another shows when downloading is complete.

7 ▷ After downloading the driver file, double-clicking it starts the install program. Follow the on-screen instructions to complete the process.

44 LOGGING ON PROCEDURE

Whichever FTP program you have installed on your computer, you must follow the same basic procedure to log on to an FTP site. You need to supply the following information:

- Site Address: this can include information about the directories on the site. Use the full address if you know it, and if your FTP program allows; otherwise use the main site address and navigate to the directory you require.
- User Name: when a user name is requested, type **anonymous**.

A quick-start FTP connection button.

45 USING ANONYMOUS FTP

When you want to transfer a file from a remote site, you must first log on to that computer. Most FTP sites simplify the procedure by having a special user account, which can be accessed by anybody. When asked for your user name, simply type in **anonymous**.

46 RECOGNIZING FILE TYPES

FTP sites contain numerous different types of files that have different extensions. These tell you, at a glance, what the files contain.

Some files may be compressed or encoded, and will require special applications to decompress them or make their contents available.

◁ IMAGES
Common image file extensions are: jpg, gif, tif, bmp, ped.

◁ AUDIO
Among the most common audio file formats are wav, mid, voc, au.

◁ VIDEO
Video file extensions include avi, mov, dl, gr, mpg.

◁ PROGRAMS
File extensions for application programs include com, exe, bat.

◁ COMPRESSED FILES
Extensions used for compressed files include zip, lzh, gz, Z, zoo, arj.

◁ TEXT
Common text extensions are txt, doc, ps, eps, htm, html.

47 MOVING AROUND AN FTP SITE

Once you have logged on to an FTP site, you may wish to explore the contents, or you may be looking for a particular file. In any case, first read any "help", "readme", or "index" files on the server. The illustration below shows how to use *CuteFTP* to access directories and files on an FTP site, but most FTP programs are similar.

Download	Ctrl+PgDn
Upload	Ctrl+PgUp
View	Ctrl+W
Edit	
Execute	Ctrl+E

△ **VIEWING TEXT FILES**
To view text files such as "index", "readme", or "help", highlight file and simply choose View from Commands menu.

To move up *to a higher directory, double-click this symbol. It does not appear when you are in server's top-level (root) directory.*

The status box *provides information about the status of the current FTP session: for example, the progress of file transfer.*

Toolbar buttons *access the most commonly used functions of the program fast, and use similar icons to Internet Explorer.*

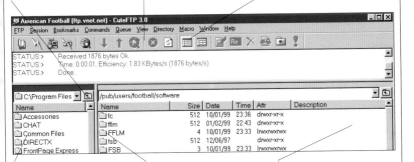

The left-hand panel *relates to the hard disk. Set up a new download folder to save files transferred from the Internet.*

To move down a directory *and view the contents, double-click on the selected folder icon in the right-hand panel.*

The right-hand panel *relates to the FTP server. Navigate to the folder from which you plan to download files to your hard disk.*

48 USING ANTIVIRUS PROGRAMS

To protect your computer from viruses, be sure to scan every file that you download with one of the many powerful antivirus programs that are available as freeware and shareware (*Tip 42*) on the Internet.

VIRUS ALERT

THE WORLD WIDE WEB

49 WHAT IS THE WORLD WIDE WEB?

Considered by many users to be the most exciting aspect of the Internet, the World Wide Web is certainly the fastest-growing area, with over 50 million Web pages to visit, and thousands more appearing every month.

The Web is a universe of pages containing text, images, sounds, and video clips. Each page is linked to other pages. The Web can also be used to retrieve files and documents from other types of Internet site.

The Web is based on Hypertext Mark-up Language (HTML). This computer programming language was developed during the 1980s by Tim Berners-Lee, who first had the idea of creating an electronic web of research information.

◁ VERY BEST OF THE WEB
For an up-to-date directory of the best Web sites, click Best of the Web *on the start page of* Microsoft Internet Explorer.

Web of linked documents contains text, images, sounds, video clips, and commercial activity.

50 WHAT CAN YOU USE THE WEB FOR?

The pages of the Web cover a vast range of topics, presented in an attractive, interesting, and easily accessible form. The information is interactive, so navigating the Web is similar to using a multimedia CD-ROM – clicking on a "live" area takes you to a new, related screen. Some of the most entertaining Web sites are those run by fans, and whatever your interests, you will find a site somewhere run by a fellow enthusiast.

COMMERCIAL ACTIVITY ▷
As businesses have recognized the huge customer base that the Web accesses, sites advertising new products or offering home shopping have begun to proliferate.

University of
Oxford
Libraries

Electronic Resources
in Oxford

◁ RESEARCH
Many academic, government, and commercial bodies publish authoritative and reliable material on the Web, making it a very useful tool for anyone involved in research.

◁ OFFICIAL SITES
National and local government are beginning to use the Web to distribute official information, including briefing papers, press releases, and even Acts of Parliament.

51 E-MAIL VIA THE WEB

If your on-line activity is centred around the Web, you will probably find it convenient to use the e-mail facility in your Web browser. For example, *Netscape Communicator* has its own mail program, which allows you to access the mail window by choosing the *Messenger* option in the *Communicator* menu.

52 SURFING THE WEB

It's easy to surf the Web, but you may be daunted by the volume of material available. Netscape's site has two pages that make good starting points for you to get a feel for what is out there: they are What's New and What's Cool. You can get to both using links on the home page at **http://www. netscape.com.**

53 WHAT HAPPENS ON A WEB PAGE?

Web pages range from quite simple, text-only, static documents to adventurous sites containing animation, sound, and interactive elements. Many Web pages allow you to download pictures, sounds, and video clips, as well as files and software, and most contain links to related pages on the same or other Web sites. Many pages also contain e-mail addresses, enabling you to contact the producer of the page.

WHAT IS A TYPICAL WEB PAGE?
Although there is no such thing as a typical Web page, the one on the right is a good example of a colourful, well-organized site. It contains textual and graphical links to other pages, an up-to-date news service, guides to eating, drinking, cinema, and other London-based activities, and even has on-line maps.

Images and text items often provide links to other Web pages or sites. Some images, such as maps, may contain several links. You can usually tell when an object is a link, as your mouse cursor will change shape to a pointing hand when it is moved over a "hot" area.

Text with links to other pages is often indicated by being underlined or shown in a different colour from the main text.

A WELL-ORGANIZED WEB PAGE

54 HOW TO IDENTIFY A WEB SITE

A Web site is distinguished by the prefix **http://** in its address. Http, which is short for HyperText Transport Protocol, refers to the standard method of transferring documents that have been created with HyperText Mark-up Language (HTML) between Web servers and browsers. Each Web site has a unique address, known as a URL.

WEB ADDRESSES
Be careful when you enter Web addresses manually. These never contain spaces and are sensitive to punctuation and case. Some contain capital letters, but they are usually lower case.

www *indicates the name of a designated Web server. Although there are many possible variations, it is standard practice to name the Web server "www".*

/home.html *denotes the directory path on the server. Here the file name is "home" and the final extension indicates that the file is an HTML file.*

http://www.superserve.com/home.html

http:// *indicates to your browser that you are connecting to a Web document. The letters "http" are always followed by a colon and two forward slashes, as illustrated in this example.*

.superserve *is the name of the host or domain. This is the commercial organization on whose computer the particular Web page resides.*

.com *(in this example) indicates that* superserve *is a commercial enterprise. The final suffix, known as the zone name, indicates the nature of the organization.*

55 THE ROLE OF HYPERTEXT

The term "hypertext" refers to text containing links to other pieces of text, either within the same document or in another one. Most Web pages are based on HyperText Mark-up Language, which is a set of codes that can be inserted into documents to control the layout and to create links to related topics in other documents.

56 WHAT IS A WEB BROWSER?

A Web browser is simply a program that enables a computer to download and view pages of the Web. However, browsers have now developed into sophisticated launchpads for most Internet activities. Two of the most popular versions are *Netscape Navigator* from Netscape Corporation and *Microsoft Internet Explorer*.

The Address box displays the URL (Uniform Resource Locator) of the site that is currently open in Internet Explorer.

Basic functions are easy to access from the start page. Access further features from menus and Options dialog boxes.

Click the Links button to access a toolbar providing links to support pages and information about new Web sites.

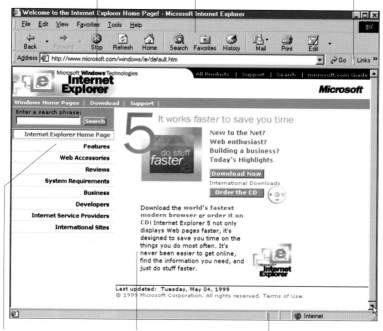

The main browser window shows the pages that make up the Web. Coloured or underlined text indicates "hot" links.

Click tabs on the home page to access directories of Web sites, information about Microsoft and Internet Explorer, etc.

The status bar shows information about the current Web page, such as the names of image files being downloaded.

57 CHANGING YOUR OPTIONS

You can speed up *Microsoft Internet Explorer* just by changing your options and choosing not to load particular types of file automatically. Choose *Internet Options* from the *Tools* menu, click on the *Advanced* tab, and scroll down to *Multimedia*. Now you can choose *not* to play sounds, or display images, videos, or animations.

HELP THIS WEB BROWSER RUN FASTER

58 BOOKMARK YOUR FAVOURITE PAGES

During your Web-browsing sessions, you may visit dozens of sites, and will inevitably require some means of noting the pages to which you wish to return. Most Web browsers include a bookmark feature that you can access quickly, and which usually allows you to organize your bookmarks into a hierarchical drop-down menu. In *Microsoft Internet Explorer*, such markers are known as "favorites".

MICROSOFT INTERNET EXPLORER FAVORITES
Managing "favorites" using Microsoft Internet Explorer is similar to managing folders in Windows 98. Because you are prompted to file new entries as you create them, minimal management is required.

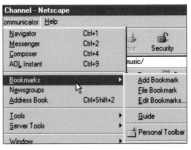

NETSCAPE NAVIGATOR BOOKMARKS
If you keep the Bookmarks window open during a Web session, you can manage your bookmarks as you proceed. New entries can be dropped directly into a folder with the Quick Link feature.

59 MULTIMEDIA ON THE WEB

The latest technologies have transformed Web pages from static pages to multimedia creations of sound, movement, and interactive links that you can access from a Web browser. All browsers can display HTML-formatted text and most image files, but the latest versions of *Netscape Navigator* and *Microsoft Internet Explorer* can also automatically handle a number of audio, video, and 3-D file formats. Browsers can be enhanced to handle additional file types by downloading and installing browser plug-ins (*Tip 60*).

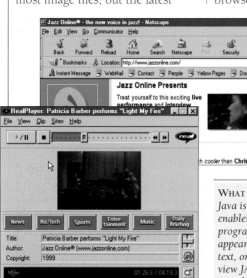

STREAMED SOUND
Many pages contain "streamed" sound files that you can listen to as they download. The Independent Underground Music Archive *at* **http:// www.iuma.com** *offers sound files in several formats, for example.*

WHAT IS JAVA?
Java is a programming language that enables Web pages to contain miniature programs (known as applets) that appear as animation, sound, scrolling text, or interactive features. In order to view JAVA applets, your Web browser must be JAVA-enhanced.

△ **STREAMED VIDEO**
Some of the newer Web browsers handle streamed video by playing a little at a time as it is received over the Internet.

This video clip of a bird in flight is displayed using Iterated Systems' CoolFusion *plug-in for* Netscape Navigator – *technology now included in* Real Networks' RealPlayer.

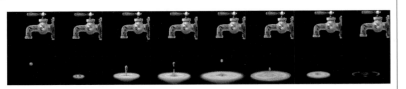

△ ANIMATED SEQUENCE
This sequence was produced using the animated GIF (GIF 89a) format. Using this format, you can put a sequence of images into a single file like frames of a cartoon film. The animation will be run automatically by the Web browser when the page containing the file is accessed.

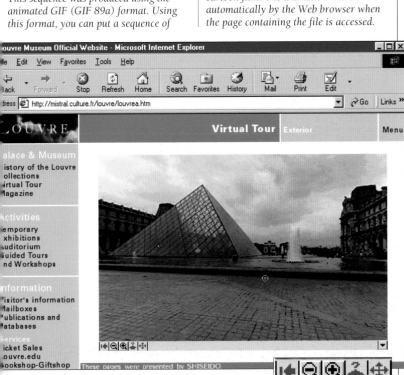

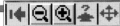

△ THREE-DIMENSIONAL GRAPHICS
Virtual Reality plug-ins like Apple's QuickTime VR *let you explore virtual worlds and manipulate three-dimensional images on the Net. This example shows one of a series of "virtual tours" on the Louvre Web site at* **http://mistral.culture.fr/louvre/louvrea.htm**.

△ NAVIGATING IN 3-D
The controls let you zoom in and out of the image, show any "hot spot" buttons, or retrace your path.

45

60 WHAT ARE PLUG-INS?

A plug-in is a program that adds features to a Web browser so that it can handle files containing different elements, such as 3-D and multimedia. You can download new plug-ins and upgrades for existing ones, usually from the software developer's home page. Keep in touch with new developments by visiting one of the regularly updated plug-in lists on the Web.

PREINSTALLED PLUG-INS
The latest versions of Netscape Navigator *and* Microsoft Internet Explorer *come with some preinstalled plug-ins.* Internet Explorer *offers a movie player called* ActiveMovie, *for example.*

AUDIO & VIDEO

Crescendo
A free plug-in from LiveUpdate that allows you to play stereo MIDI music from the Web, with a CD-like control panel and digital counter.

IntervuMPEG Player
Intervu's plug-in lets you play MPEG audio-video files that are streamed as you download them. You can preview the first frame before downloading it.

RapidTransit
Fastman's RapidTransit decompresses and plays high-quality stereo sound from Web pages.

3D & ANIMATION

CosmoPlayer
Produced by Silicon Graphics, CosmoPlayer is a VRML viewer.

Live Picture Viewer
This viewer lets you see 3D objects and panoramic images from all angles.

Superscape Viscape Universal
This 3D plug-in lets you explore 3-D worlds in both VRML and Superscape's own SVR formats.

Wirl Virtual Reality Browser
This is an advanced VRML plug-in from Vream.

OTHER PLUG-INS

Earthtime
Starfish Software's plug-in lets you view the time around the world. The animated map indicates daylight and darkness.

GrafixView
InfoMill's GrafixView displays tiff, png, bmp, and jpg graphic formats in a separate browser window with fast image manipulation tools.

PLUG-INS

61 SEARCHING THE WEB

The possibility of finding exactly what you are looking for among the millions of individual Web pages might appear unlikely. However, powerful search tools are available that will trawl Web sites and newsgroups, searching for your chosen criteria, and return results very quickly, usually within seconds. The two main types of search tool available to use are search engines and Web directories.

62 USING THE ALTAVISTA SEARCH ENGINE

AltaVista is one of the most popular search engines. To use it, open your Web browser (in this case *Netscape Navigator*) and type the address **http://www.altavista.com**. You can then type in what you are searching for.

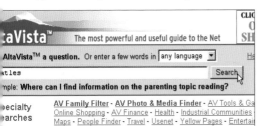

1 △ Clicking the *Search* button in *Navigator's* toolbar leads to *Netscape's* search page, which can redirect you to *Excite*, *Lycos*, *Infoseek* and others. There are even UK-specific search sites on the list.

2 ◁ Typing a word in *Altavista's* search box trawls the indexes for Web pages with that word. It usually takes more than one word to narrow it down.

3 ▷ *AltaVista* tells you how many sites were found, listing first ten in window. To visit any of these, right-click on page title or address; choose *Open in New Window.*

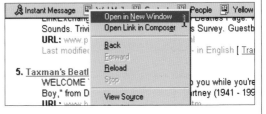

4 ◁ After viewing page, close Web browser window. You can now return to *AltaVista* page displayed in first browser window.

10. **Music Boulevard Discography: The Beatles**
The Beatles Singles Pages presents... back to The
Artist: By Album: By Song: Or Search Classical B
URL: www.musicblvd.com/cgi-bin/tw/29748_42_00
Last modified 16-Apr-99 - page size 303K - in Engl

Result Pages: 1 2 3 4 5 6 7 8 9 10 11 12 13 14 15
word count: beatles: 546459

5 △ To look at next page of ten sites relating to your search criterion, scroll to bottom of screen. Click on 2.

63 ALL-IN-ONE SEARCH PAGES

A search page provides a direct link to many of the major search engines and directories. Two of the best are provided by Netscape at **http://www.netscape.com/home/internet-search.html** and Microsoft at **http://www.msn.com/search/ie5/searchsetup.asp**.

64 USING A WEB DIRECTORY

Some search engines like Yahoo! and Lycos categorize their indexes to make it easier for you to find what you're interested in. This cuts down the problem of irrelevant search results, where search engines produce masses of pages outside your area of interest. If you type "Chippendale" into a general search engine you'll get references to towns and individuals as well as to the historical furniture.

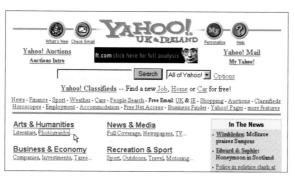

1 ◁ On the opening page of Yahoo!'s UK & Ireland site at *http://www.yahoo.co.uk*, it shows the highest level of categories, with links to some of their subcategories.

2 ◁ Choosing Photography from the *Arts & Humanities* section shows a first selection of possible pages, with subcategories.

3 ▷ Under the section Photographers, choosing *Masters* gets you to named photographers.

65 RESTRICTING YOUR SEARCH

Categorized search engines let you narrow down the search by location as well as by information type. So at Yahoo!, for example, it is possible to restrict your search to sites in the UK and Ireland if you want to find a local supplier of information or products.

4 ▷ Choose *Lewis Carroll* from the list of photographic *Masters* to reach a Web site dedicated to his work.

- Carroll, Lewis (1832-1898)@ 🏴
- Goldsworthy, Andy (1956-)@ 🏴
- Muybridge, Eadweard (1830-1904)@ 🏴

- Livick, Stephen (1945-) NEW!

5 ◁ The site's home page provides a list of Carroll's photographs available on-line, as well as background information.

Rev. Charles Lutwidge Dodgson

aka Lewis Carroll

Photo grapher

Here is a small set of photos. Eventually we want to do something interesting here -

page is in memory of Helmut Gernsheim who made Dodgson's photography known t who, over the years, has taught us so much about the early days of ph

are two round robins. The second is for Alice and the first for the others. At the the upper right takes you to the other set

Aileen Wilson-Todd, taken a Croft Rectory (CD's family home).
Mr. and Mrs. Millais with their two daughters.
Alice Constance Westmacott, daughter of the sculptor Richard Westmacott
Two Children - *Museum of the History of Science, Oxford*
Beatrice Henley - daughter of the Vicar of Putney.
Ellen Terry - actress at 18 (already disastrously married).
Florence Puckersmith - daughter of the Bishop of Ripon.
Marcus Keane.
Maria White, niece of the porter at Lambeth Palace.
Dante Gabriel Rossetti, poet and painter
Christina Rossetti and her mother.
Alexander Munro, sculptor, with his wife.
Hallam Tennyson, son of Alfred, Lord Tennyson.
Alfred, Lord Tennyson

D. Gabriel Rossetti
Oct 6 1863

6 ▷ The final result of the search: the photograph of Dante Gabriel Rossetti by Lewis Carroll that you'd found referred to in an art history textbook but never previously seen.

LOGGING ON WITH TELNET

66 UNDERSTANDING TELNET

One of the oldest Internet activities, Telnet is a program that allows you to log on to a remote computer and access services there from your PC. Although not all Telnet sites are free, some research organizations, universities, and libraries offer free access. You control a Telnet session from your keyboard, choosing options from a list, and typing a number or a letter to access a series of menu screens – a little like using an old-fashioned terminal at a public library.

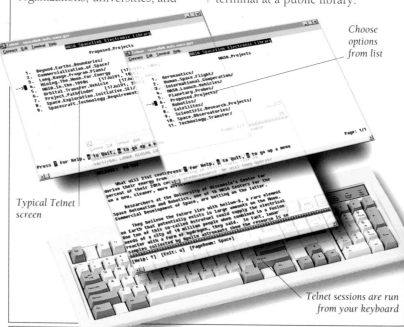

Choose options from list

Typical Telnet screen

Telnet sessions are run from your keyboard

67 ACCESSING TELNET WITH WINDOWS® 98

You can access Telnet in two main ways – using *Windows 98* or via the Web – but in either case, you will need to install Telnet software on your PC. This is supplied with *Windows 98*, or can be downloaded from an Internet software site such as **http://www.winfiles.com**. To log on with *Windows 98*, first double-click on the Telnet icon in the *Windows* folder.

1 △ To access a *Telnet* site, choose *Remote System* from *Connect* menu.

USING TELNET
Most people use Telnet to access on-line databases, or to read articles and books on-line. It is also possible to use Telnet to play on-line games and to run other programs. The examples shown are from the Stone Keep bulletin board system, a user-administered site.

2 ◁ Type name of site you wish to access in *Host Name* panel of *Connect* box, then click *Connect* button. When you are connected to site, login screen will appear.

```
Telnet - bbs.stonekeep.net
Connect  Edit  Terminal  Help
/ïÄÄÄÄÄ-ÄÄ-Ä-ÄÄ-ÄÄÄ-ÄÄÄÄ-Ä - ù . ú        ú . ù - Ä-ÄÄÄÄ-ÄÄÄ-ÄÄ-Ä-ÄÄ-ÄÄÄÄÄÄ
Enter your alias, real name or enter "New" to log on as a new user.
Name: New

Login as a new user? [No]: Yes



Welcome! You have chosen to logon as a new user. Your information will be
kept STRICTLY CONFIDENTIAL, and will never be seen except by administration
of this system or at the request of a legal subpoena.

You will be required to answer several newuser questions, the answers to
which will be recorded in your user record. If you wish to continue
logging in as a new user, please respond YES to the next question. If you
have decided you do not wish to be a member, respond NO and you will be
promptly logged off.

Thanks,
Justin Boxberger - Stone Keep

Continue login as new user? [Yes]: █
```

3 ▷ Once connected, follow on-screen instructions. In this example, you answer **Yes** when asked if you want to log on as a new user, and receive a message from the site manager about confidentiality.

68 CAN'T FIND WINDOWS® 98 TELNET PROGRAM?

Access *Find* utility from *Start* menu, choose *Files or Folders*, type **Telnet** in *Named* box, and click OK. Right-click on Telnet icon when it appears and drag on to desktop. Release mouse button over desktop and choose *Create Shortcut(s)* from menu that appears.

69 ACCESSING TELNET WITH A WEB BROWSER

As well as using *Windows 98* to access Telnet, you can configure your Web browser to launch your Telnet client automatically when you click on a link to a Telnet site, or when you type in a URL starting **telnet://**. To configure *Netscape Navigator*, for example, follow the steps below and the next time you access a Telnet site, the Telnet software will be launched automatically.

1 △ From *Edit* menu in main *Navigator* window, choose *Preferences*. The *Preferences* dialog box will appear.

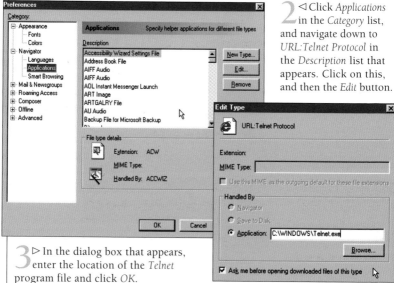

2 ◁ Click *Applications* in the *Category* list, and navigate down to *URL:Telnet Protocol* in the *Description* list that appears. Click on this, and then the *Edit* button.

3 ▷ In the dialog box that appears, enter the location of the *Telnet* program file and click *OK*.

70 READ THE INSTRUCTIONS

Telnet sites are not all organized in the same way, so it is important to read very carefully the instructions in the opening menu screens when you log on. If you are experiencing difficulties, you can usually call up a help menu by typing **H** or **?** or **help** at any time. If you are really stuck, type **exit** or **logout** to end the session.

NEWSGROUPS ON THE INTERNET

71 WHAT ARE NEWSGROUPS?

Newsgroups on the Internet have little to do with "news", but instead provide a unique opportunity for public discussion and debate. Participants "post" messages that are available to all readers of the newsgroup, who can then choose to reply – either publicly or privately – to the message. The messages can include sounds, images, or video clips. Newsgroups thus provide a forum for interested parties to discuss topics of mutual interest, and offer some of the most stimulating content on the Internet.

POSTED MESSAGES

NETSCAPE NEWSREADER
The Netscape Navigator *Web browser has a built-in newsreader that makes it easy to access newsgroups.*

72 THE USENET NETWORK

Usenet is the name given to the huge body of newsgroups that are distributed around the world by computers known as "news servers". These servers exchange information so that each one carries a copy of the most recent messages. Usenet is not part of the Internet, although Internet sites are used to carry its newsgroups. If you are not linked to the Internet, you can still access newsgroups by dialling a BBS that carries Usenet.

73 NEWSGROUP CLASSIFICATIONS

Newsgroups in the Usenet network are classified according to subject, with about 20 top-level (major subject) categories. Names of newsgroups, like e-mail addresses, follow a hierarchical structure, with the prefix indicating the top-level classification category.

◁ **NEWS**
Look here first if you are new to Usenet. Over 20 groups dealing with the network, including useful software, new groups, and advice. Try **news.announce.newuser**

MISC ▷
Over 100 assorted groups ranging from pension funds to bodybuilding. Try **misc.invest.stocks**

TALK ▷

More than 20 newsgroups that provide a forum for debate on any topic, especially the more controversial ones. Try **talk.euthanasia**

COMP ▷
Over 750 computer-oriented groups, including technical advice. Try **comp.sys.ibm.pc.games. adventure**

△ **BIZ**
Over 60 business groups, where marketing and advertising are acceptable activities. Try **biz.jobs.offered** *or* **biz.comp.services**

▽ **SOC**
More than 200 groups concerned with a variety of social, cultural, and religious issues, including the environment, politics, and socializing. Try **soc. rights.human**

▽ **ALT**
Over 2,500 "alternative" groups discussing everything from New Age remedies to independent music. Try **alt.astrology** *or* **alt.music.beatles**

 ◁ **REC**
Over 550 groups devoted to recreational activities, including most of the arts. Try **rec.sport.triathlon**

SCI ▷
Over 150 groups interested in scientific debate, and research and development. Try **sci.virtual world**

74 NEWSGROUPS OUTSIDE USENET

There are some newsgroups outside the Usenet umbrella, but they tend to be concerned mainly with local issues. For example, some service providers set up their own local newsgroups in order to enable their subscribers to share information about the service, but these groups are not necessarily distributed to other news servers.

75 SUBSCRIBING TO A NEWSGROUP

To participate in a newsgroup, you must first subscribe to it. This means that you need to tell your news reading program – the one built into *Netscape Communicator*, for instance – which news server you want to download messages from, and which newsgroups you are interested in. The newsreader will then download a number of message headers from the most recent messages in each group you join, and you can then download the full text of any messages you want to read or respond to. You can choose how many to download.

1 ◁ Click *Newsgroup Servers* in *Communicator's Preferences* box. This will let you enter the name of the news server you want to use – your service provider will have given you the name of their own server.

2 ▷ Click on *Messenger* in the *Communicator* menu, and then click on the news server's name in the left-hand panel. Then click *Subscribe* in the *File* menu.

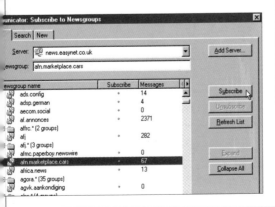

3 ◁ Choose newsgroups you want to subscribe to from the list in the *Subscribe* window. These will appear in the main *Messenger* window.

76 POSTING MESSAGES

Messages (sometimes known as articles) sent to a newsgroup are said to be "posted", as they address a group rather than an individual. There are various ways of doing this. In these steps you can see how to follow up a newsgroup message that you are currently reading, using the newsreader in *Netscape Communicator*.

1 ▷ Click *New Msg* in the *Messenger* toolbar. A message window will appear with the address of the current group.

2 ◁ Type a subject for the message you want to post to the group. This is the header that other readers of the newsgroup will see.

3 ▷ If responding to a message, the original text will be copied to the new window. You can edit to include the points you are responding to.

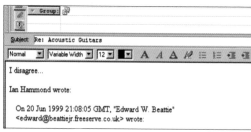

CENSORING MATERIAL
If you are concerned about children accessing unsuitable material, seek advice from your service provider or dealer about software for blocking such information.

4 ◁ Click *Send* button. Message will be posted to newsgroup, and e-mail will be sent to the author of the message you are responding to.

77 REPLYING PRIVATELY TO A MESSAGE

It is considered courteous to reply personally (by sending an e-mail) as well as publicly to the author of a message that has been posted to a newsgroup. However, if you prefer to reply only privately, you can do this by sending an e-mail directly to that person.

78 How to Behave in Newsgroups

Although there are no hard-and-fast rules about how to behave in newsgroups, a voluntary code has grown up with the Usenet network. If you are a newcomer, try to familiarize yourself with these guidelines in order to avoid irritating regular users by barging into discussion without preparation, or by posting irrelevant questions.

> **LURKING**
> "Lurk" in a newsgroup for a few days before joining so you can find out what the group's concerns are, whether they interest you, and the level at which postings should be pitched.

79 Newsgroup Netiquette

The basic principle behind newsgroup netiquette is simply to maintain an awareness of other members of the Usenet and their needs. Bear this in mind and your experiences should be enjoyable.

- **Read the FAQ**
Many newsgroups produce a document containing answers to Frequently Asked Questions. Read this to avoid troubling the group with basic questions.

- **Be Relevant**
Newsgroups often deal with a narrow range of issues, so make sure that your message is relevant.

- **Be Descriptive**
Give your posting a descriptive title to help members choose which articles to read.

- **Be Careful with Humour**
Humour and irony are difficult to convey in written communication so back up ambiguous statements with an "emoticon" (an emotional icon).

- **Avoid "Spamming"**
Posting identical messages to many groups (known as spamming) is frowned upon and may invoke rough justice. For example, spammers may find themselves mail-bombed by thousands of pieces of junk e-mail.

- **Don't be Rude**
If you are irritated by a posting, send a private e-mail rather than conduct an argument in public.

- **Be Brief**
Express yourself in a clear manner and keep your posting concise.

GOOD CONDUCT

PLAYING GAMES ON-LINE

80 WHAT IS ON-LINE GAMING?

The new generation of computer games has quickly adapted to the wired world. Almost every new game released has a network option, where players can compete over a local network or the Internet. Players too have adapted to the idea of competing with other human beings rather than with the PC's limited artificial intelligence. All kinds of games, from shoot 'em ups like *Quake* to strategy games like *Command* and *Conquer*, can now be played on-line.

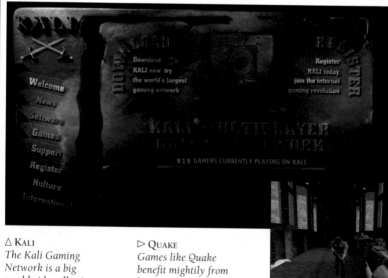

△ KALI
The Kali Gaming Network is a big worldwide collection of game servers.

▷ QUAKE
Games like Quake benefit mightily from having multiple human players online.

81 WHAT DO YOU NEED?

To get the most out of on-line gaming, you need a fast PC and the speediest Internet connection you can afford. As all current gamers know, it should have a high-speed Pentium II or III processor, lots of memory, and a 3-D accelerator graphics card. Add to that the need to download data about other players' positions and movement in multiplayer Internet games, and only the highest specification will do. You will also need an Internet account.

New to the Zone?
Start Here!

Fighter Ace: Free Trial Offer Available Now!

Free Games!
Ants (40)
Backgammon (433)
Bridge (262)
Checkers (109)

△ GAME SELECTION
Some on-line games require you to buy and install a full copy of the game on your PC. Others are free.

△ BIG SELLERS
ID Software's Doom and Quake were among the first multiplayer games.

▽ STRATEGIC CHOICE
Microsoft's Age of Empires is a real-time strategy game for multiplayer use.

UP TO SPEED
Servers keep network traffic to a minimum by sending only essential data to each player. In Quake II, for example, the graphics of the locations are handled by the players' own PCs, and all the server sends down the line are the locations and movements made by other players.

82 GAMES ETIQUETTE

In the high-speed world of modern games, etiquette is still developing. You will find games servers where new players are mercilessly ganged up on by the experts, and where the on-line note system, in which players can write messages to each other during play, is used for abusive and often obscene purposes. Look for a server that matches your skill level and your general attitude to your fellow players, stay polite, and don't crow over your victories.

83 GETTING STARTED

One way to find game servers is the GameSpy 3D utility, available to download at **http://www.gamespy.com**. This not only keeps track of which servers are on-line and directs you to the right places on the Internet, it also gives each server a "ping" rating to indicate which are busiest, and therefore slowest to respond.

△ SEEKING SERVERS
The GameSpy list of game servers is arranged by game title.

◁ GAMES CHAT
The GameSpy site has mulit-user game news and chat forums.

84 SIGNING ON TO WIREPLAY

The Wireplay service (**http://www.wireplay.co.uk**) is a popular route into on-line games. The service is free, and supports more than 100 games in two game "arenas". To join in, you download the Wireplay client software from the Web site, and sign on with your chosen nickname. The Wireplay client dials into the server.

▽ WIREPLAY CLIENT
Choose between the UK-only PowerPlay arena or worldwide OpenPlay arena.

▷ LOGGING IN
All you have to do is enter your nickname and click the Connect button.

85 PRACTICE MAKES PERFECT

You may be the best *Quake* player you know, and a demon at *HalfLife* and *Unreal*. But the on-line gaming world is very different, with many tricks and techniques to use and the danger of unpredictable human opponents who will be better than you at first. Take time to observe how the system works, how the more experienced players beat you, and practise on-line as much as you can. The only way to learn about multiplayer games is to play them, and practise, practise, practise.

86 PICKING YOUR LEVEL

Most game servers and services give you a chance to ease your way into on-line games rather than putting you immediately at the mercy of the world's best players. There are game areas restricted to beginners, as well as areas restricted to the most experienced, and it's a good idea not to be too optimistic about your prowess the first few times. Start at the bottom, and work your way up the skill level only once you're sure it won't be an embarrassment.

TERMINOLOGY
The entry-level games areas you visit might be categorised under Novices *or* Newbies, *but these games are not easy.*

ENTRY LEVEL
This Wireplay screen lets you choose the novice level, and introduces other levels with software details.

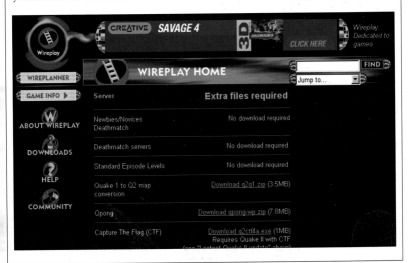

Server	Extra files required
Newbies/Novices Deathmatch	No download required
Deathmatch servers	No download required
Standard Episode Levels	No download required
Quake 1 to Q2 map conversion	Download q2q1.zip (3.5MB)
Qpong	Download qpong-wp.zip (7.8MB)
Capture The Flag (CTF)	Download q2ctf4a.exe (1MB) Requires Quake II with CTF (see "Latest Quake II update" above)

87 ACTION GAMES

Action games have always been the most popular category on-line, from the earliest multiplayer flight combat simulators to the shoot 'em ups and driving games of today. Games like *Quake II*, *Red Alert*, *Colin McRae Rally*, *Tribes*, and *HalfLife* take on a new dimension with human opponents.

▽ **RALLY DRIVER**
Colin McRae Rally pits you against the terrain as well as your opponents.

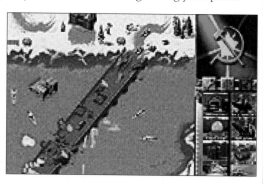

◁ **TAKE AIM**
In Quake II, watch out for on-line rivals rather than monsters.

88 STRATEGY GAMES

Strategy games like *Red Alert* and *Age of Empires* work well in multiplayer mode. You can take on the challenge of psyching out your opponent, making the unexpected move or the sneak attack, and knowing for sure that nobody has a chance of guessing your plans.

RED ALERT
Strategy, tactics, and logistics – not to mention ruthlessness – all have parts to play in Red Alert.

TURN OR REALTIME
Traditional turn-based strategy games have been overtaken by real-time games in which all the players move continuously.

89 TRADITIONAL GAMES

Some games could always be played with distant opponents, as in postal chess. But now all traditional games can be played that way, without the long turnaround times of the post service. Bridge is very popular, with many players looking for new partners to form foursomes, and other games like backgammon, cribbage, draughts, and Go all have their adherents. The on-line versions of these games are usually among the ones on offer for free download, and although their graphics might not be the flashiest, they get the game played. Those who want to improve their skills at any of these games will readily find players with various skill levels.

ON THE BOARD
Backgammon is popular for on-line gamers, with the computer providing the random element of throwing the dice and the players providing the skill.

TAKING TURNS
Turn-based games like chess and draughts are ideal for those without the latest processors and 3-D accelerated graphics boards.

90 FUTURE GAMES

The future of on-line games and game servers is clear in one way, and hazy in others. There's no doubt that every new game released will have a multiplayer or network option if at all possible, that the games will get bigger, more complex and more demanding, and that more players will want to try their hands against human adversaries. This will place even higher demands on PC speed, server performance, and Internet connections. But the real future of on-line gaming lies in the broadband technologies now emerging, such as cable modems and ADSL services. "Bigger, better, and faster" sums up the future of on-line games, just as they sum up the future of the computer itself.

USEFUL WEB SITES

91 SEARCH ENGINES & DIRECTORIES

These search tools help you navigate around the Web to find exactly what you want. Some are more discriminating than others and it is useful to get to know them so you can compare their services.

ALTAVISTA
http://www.altavista.com
Comprehensive, vast and fast, with Web and Usenet searches, it is well laid out and allows multilingual searches.

DEJANEWS
http://www.dejanews.com
Has a huge number of discussion groups plus massive archive of Usenet articles.

EXCITE
http://www.aexcite.com
A Web search database that comes in global editions with lots of the usual services. Rather ponderous.

HOTBOT
http://www.hotbot.com
Can find over 15 million e-mail addresses from around the world, and has other excellent search options.

INFOSEEK
http://www.infoseek.com
Easy-to-use Web site directory. Web search gives fast, accurate results and there are lots of other services.

LOOKSMART
http://www.looksmart.com
Attractive, easy-to-use, and fast Web search giving most popular sites.

LYCOS
http://www.lycos.com
Not as comprehensive a database as some, but has good range of services such as maps, city guides, and news.

MAGELLAN
http://www.mckinley.netcom.com
A very large directory with a useful short site review and a comprehensive range of services.

NORTHERN LIGHT
http://www.nlsearch.com
Boasts a special collection of over 5,000 books, journals, magazines, and newswires.

REGIONAL DIRECTORIES
http://www.edirectory.com
A big list, with Web directories for nearly every country and US state.

YAHOO
http://www.yahoo.com
Massive, comprehensive, easy to navigate, and reliable with plenty of interesting specialist services to use.

92 ENTERTAINMENT

There are literally thousands of sites you can visit which fall into this category, whether you just want information or you want to buy something. The sites listed below are just a few and include music, video, books and television.

ALL MUSIC GUIDE
http://www.allmusic.com
Very comprehensive music database with online ordering and related sites.

AMAZON BOOKS
http://www.amazon.com
The best-known online bookstore – 2.5 million books, plus a wide range of CDs, videos, toys and consumer electronics.

CELEBSITES
http://www.celebsites.com
Actors, models, musicians, athletes and more to find on this celebrity watch site.

RECORD FINDER
http://www.recordfinders.com
Order from an enormous selection of deleted vinyl plus vintage turntables; also related newsgroup links.

REEL
http://www.reel.com
Claims to be the best place to buy videos, with a huge number of titles.

SOAP LINKS
http://members.aol.com/soaplinks
Keep up with the latest events and strange storylines in all the soaps.

SONY
http://www.sony.com
Movies, TV, video, DVD, and shopping all on one site. Also includes a game show network.

THE ULTIMATE BAND LIST
http://www.ubl.com
Impressive directory of pop and rock bands. Look up your favourites, win concert tickets, chat, and order on-line.

TICKETMASTER
http://www.ticketmaster.com
Book tickets on-line for concerts, sports events, dance, theatre, and much more.

UK NATIONAL LOTTERY
http://lottery.merseyworld.com
Includes numerical analysis, statistics, winning numbers, and a chat room.

93 SECURE SHOPPING ON THE WEB

Concerns about transaction security have not stopped millions of customers taking advantage of the wider choice, lower prices, and general convenience of Internet shopping. Security is now handled by strong encryption protocols, and there is no more need to worry about your credit card details than there is when you read it out over the phone. All types of purchases, from a bunch of flowers to a new car or house, can be handled by an equally wide range of providers, both household names and Internet newcomers.

94 SPORTS AND GAMES

Computer games are not the only ones to feature on-line. There are news and statistics sites for every sport and pastime you can imagine, produced by enthusiastic amateurs or real professionals.

ALL ENGLAND LAWN TENNIS CLUB
http://www.wimbledon.com
Player interviews and trivia as well as scores and match results.

BOXING.COM
http://www.boxing.com
The boxing enthusiast's Web site, with fight coverage and latest bouts listed.

CHARGED
http://www.charged.com
"Extreme sports" site, with activities such as cross-country skateboarding, climbing, and snowboarding.

CRIC INFO
http://www.cricket.org
The latest cricket news in the UK, USA, India, South Africa, and Australia.

FORMULA1.COM
http://www.formula1.com
News, results, teams, circuits, and exclusive interviews with drivers.

GOLF.COM
http://www.golf.com
News, views, course directory, and information on the latest competitions around the world.

SCRUM.COM
http://www.scrum.co.uk
Fixtures, match reports, player info, and rugby reports from around the world included here.

SKICENTRAL
http://www.skicentral.com
Daily ski guide, resorts info, trip planning, and events guide.

SOCCERNET
http://www.soccernet.com
Daily Mail-run site for everything you need to know about British football.

SPORTSWEB
http://www.sportsweb.com
The lastest sports news from around the world, courtesy of Reuters.

95 COMPUTERS & SOFTWARE

As you might expect, computer-related sites are plentiful. Try typing any computer company name with **www** in front of it and **.com** afterwards, and you stand a good chance of getting through.

ADOBE
http://www.adobe.com
Information, downloads, and support for Adobe's desktop publishing programs.

APPLE
http://www.apple.com
Latest products info, updates, news, and support for Mac users.

MICROSOFT
http://www.microsoft.com
Upgrades, news, support, and more for anyone with Microsoft products.

SOFTWARE.NET
http://www.software.net
Order your software by mail order, and some of it even by e-mail at this site.

96 SCIENCE & TECHNOLOGY

The Internet has become a prime tool for scientific research, with published papers, research data, and educational material of all kinds on subjects from astronomy to zoology.

NASA
http://www.nasa.gov
Everything from the first moon missions to NASA's latest projects is here.

NEW SCIENTIST
http://www.newscientist.com
Features, news, letters, jobs, and back issues.

NETSURFER SCIENCE
http://www.netsurf.com/nss
Subscribe to receive weekly bulletins on science and technology sites.

POPSCI
http://www.popsci.com
From Popular Science magazine, all that is new and exciting in the world of science and technology.

THE LAB
http://www.abc.net.au/science
Science news, features, and fun from the Australian Broadcasting Corporation.

VOLCANO WORLD
http://.volcano.und.nodak.edu
Watch volcanoes erupting, see pictures of major volcanoes worldwide, and ask volcanologists questions on-line.

97 THE ARTS

You can take virtual tours of the world's great art and literature collections, with no charge apart from your telephone bill. See treasures you may never get around to visiting in real life.

MUSEUM OF MODERN ART NY
http://www.moma.org
Includes the collection, exhibitions, programs, and events and publications.

SHAKESPEARE'S GLOBE
http://www.reading.ac.uk/globe
The original Globe, the Globe rebuilt, and performances and news bulletin.

SMITHSONIAN INSTITUTION
http://www.si.edu
Sixteen museums and one zoo are represented on this huge Web site.

THE BRITISH LIBRARY
http://portico.bl.uk
Just a taster of the British Library's contents plus info on services.

THE NATIONAL GALLERY
http://www.nationalgallery.org.uk
See the collection and exhibitions; search for a painting and what's new.

WEBMUSEUM
http://sunsite.doc.ic.ac.uk/wm
A collection of artworks from many different sources around the world.

WORLD WIDE ART RESOURCES
http://wwar.world-arts-resources.com
Huge index of the arts, from music and photography to architecture and painting.

98 HEALTH

Look up the scientific data and trial results of any prescription drug on the market. Find a support group for a particular medical condition. Or get some advice on diet and exercise. It's all on-line.

ACHOO
http://www.achoo.com
A huge and easy-to-use directory of healthcare problems.

AMERICAN HEART ASSOCIATION
http://www.justmove.org
Advice on activities to reduce the risk of heart disease and stroke.

THRIVE
http://thriveonline.com
Get back to fitness on this site, with medical advice, exercise programmes, and healthy recipes to keep you fit.

VIRTUAL HOSPITAL
http://www.vh.org
A site for "apprentice learners", that is, patients and healthcare workers.

WORLD HEALTH ORGANIZATION
http://www.who.int
Information on the work of the WHO, including research papers, references, and info on the Director General.

YOGA
http://www.timages.com/yoga.htm
How to get in shape using yoga, with a personalized routine.

99 FOOD & DRINK

For gourmets the whole world over, the Web is a prime source of recipes, restaurant reviews, background information, and almost everything else to do with enjoying the best things in life.

BEN AND JERRY'S
http://www.benjerry.com
Ice cream by mail, customer assistance, gifts, and games are on offer here.

CHOCOLATE LOVER'S PLAYGROUND
http://www.godiva.com
A chocaholic's heaven, but on-line ordering only if you are in the USA.

CAMPBELL'S SOUP COMPANY
http://www.campbellsoups.com
As well as product and nutrition info, learn how to make a soup into a tasty meal.

RESTAURANT ROW
http://www.restaurantrow.com
Find relevant eateries worldwide by keying in your food preferences.

SMIRNOFF
http://www.smirnoff.com
A site for those of legal drinking age, with over 365 cocktail recipes.

TEA HEALTH
http://www.teahealth.co.uk
Types of tea, info for health professionals, and research library.

TESCO ONLINE
http://www.tesco.co.uk
Order your weekly groceries from the supermarket's Web site or just browse.

100 GARDENS & GARDENING

This traditional British enthusiasm is well-supported by the on-line world. Get advice, information, and new ideas for your garden, whether you have a window box or the grounds of a grand home to cultivate.

BRITISH TREES
http://www.u-net.com/trees/home.htm
Conservation, forestry, dendrology, and relevant publications on British trees.

GARDENING.COM
http://www.gardening.com
Includes a gardening encyclopedia, problem solver, and garden design info.

NATURAL HISTORY BOOKSHOP
http://www.nhbs.co.uk
Over 60,000 titles you can browse or search on all things environmental.

ROYAL HORTICULTURAL SOCIETY
http://www.address.com
Plant database, details on all gardening events, plus links to other garden sites.

THE NATIONAL TRUST
http://www.nationaltrust.org.uk
Gardens to visit, memberships details, news and events, plus NT gifts.

THE VIRTUAL GARDEN
http://www.pathfinder.com/vg
Huge horticultural digest with details of magazines, databases, and directories.

101 TRAVEL & WEATHER

Book your flight and hotel on-line, or check out your holiday destination and its climate before you pack the wrong clothes. Or just check the weather with friends abroad. The information is out there.

EASYJET
http://www.easyjet.co.uk
No-frills European flights at very competitive prices. Book on-line.

LONELY PLANET GUIDEBOOKS
http://www.lonelyplanet.com.au
Basic travel info on all countries in the series, plus book ordering on-line.

MICROSOFT EXPEDIA
http://www.expedia.msn.co.uk
Allows you to book a holiday, flights, and accommodation plus car rental.

ROUGH GUIDES
http://www.roughguides.com
Complete coverage of over 10,000 destinations. Flight and car rental.

THE MET OFFICE
http://www.met-office.gov.uk
Definitive site for the UK, giving weather and forecast information.

WORLD CLIMATE
http://www.worldclimate.com
Do a name search and get detailed info on weather and geographical location.

INDEX

ACKNOWLEDGMENTS

Dorling Kindersley would like to thank Liz Granger for compiling the index, Anna Hayman for editorial help, Louise Paddick for DTP assistance, and Andy Sansom for picture research.

Photography

KEY: t *top*; b *below*; c *centre*; a *above*; l *left*; r *right*

The publisher would like to thank the following for their kind permission to reproduce their photographs: Cyberia Paris, one of Cyberia's global chain of Internet cafés, photo/Frederik Fourment 22cl; Robert Harding Picture Library/Warren Faidley 5tr; The Image Bank/Garry Gay 5tr; NASA/JPL 1, 5bc, 7tr, 31br, 50; NCSA/UIUC 11tr; Copyright © 1996 PhotoDisc, Inc. 2; Telegraph Colour Library 36br, 54bl.

Illustrations

The publisher would like to thank the following copyright holders for their kind permission to reproduce their screengrabs/products all of which are trademarks: 3com/U.S. Robotics 12r; Altavista Company, all rights reserved: 47c; Amazon.com is a registered trademark of Amazon.com Inc. of the United States and other countries. Copyright 1996-1999 Amazon.com Inc: 65tr; © Associated Newspapers: 40; Copyright © 1994-1999 CDNOW, Inc. All rights reserved: 47bl; Copyright © 1995-1999 CNET, Inc. All rights reserved: 30tr, 32l, 34l, b; Copyright © 1995-1998 Creative Labs, Inc: 32r; Department of Trade and Industry: 39cr; Copyright © 1998 Diamond Multimedia Systems Inc: 35t, c; Copyright © 1999 GameSpy Industries: 60t; HotBot is a registered trademark of Wired Venture Inc, the parent company of Wired Digital Inc. Copyright © 1994-99 Wired Digital Inc. All rights reserved: 64tr; id software: 58ca; jazzonline.com: 44c; reproduced by kind permission of Kali Inc: 58; Copyright © 1999 Lycos, Inc. All rights reserved. Lycos® is a registered trademark of Carnegie Mellon University: 64tr; Magellan, Copyright © 1998 The McKinley Group, Inc., a subsidiary of Excite Inc. All rights reserved: 64r; MSN is a trademark, and Microsoft, MS DOS, Windows and Internet Explorer are registered trademarks of Microsoft Corporation. Screen shots reprinted with permission from Microsoft Corporation: 13t, 16-17, 18-19, 25tr, 26-27, 28-29, 35b, 37c, 42, 43bl, tr, 51, 52, 59cb; Motorola Multimedia Group: 14b; Musee du Louvre, Paris: 45b; Copyright © 1999 Netscape Communications Corporation. Netscape Communications Corporation has not authorised, sponsored or endorsed, or approved this publication and is not responsible for its content. Netscape and the Netscape Communications Corporate logos are trademarks and trade names of Netscape Communications Corporation. All other product names and/or logos are trademarks of their respective owners. 10, 30b, 43br, 47b, 53b, 55, 56: Copyright © 1997-1999, Northern Light Technology LLC. All rights reserved: 64l; Copyright © RealNetworks, Inc and/or its licensors, all rights reserved: 44clb, 10b; Tesco Online: 39tr; University of Oxford Libraries: 39cl; Copyright © 1999 Wireplay: 61b; Yahoo! is a trademark of Yahoo! Inc. Copyright © 1994-99 Yahoo! All Rights Reserved; 48c.

Every effort has been made to trace the copyright holders. The publisher apologizes for any unintentional omissions and would be pleased, in such cases, to place an acknowledgment in future editions.